Vibration Of Words

A Poetry Book By:

Jamal DuBois Simmons

Dedication

This book is dedicated to my father. The first person I remember receiving positive words from. He was sure to speak life into a young me. King Jay, a phrase used to address me. How could I not be King.

Preface

Words are sounds that carry energy. All sounds have a natural power through their own frequency. When we speak, our words vibrate from low to high frequencies because they hold vibration. The weight, sound, and appearance of words have the power to affect us positively or negatively. Be sure to use words that raise your vibration daily.

Table Of Contents

1. I Ain't No Poet
2. Remember He Said
3. Holler To The Mountain Top
4. Have Mercy
5. The Letter P
6. Pretty Tony
7. Words From The Homey
8. Real Nigga Poetry
9. Father Figure
10. Manhood
11. Follow Through
12. Baptized In Lake Minnetonka
13. Ashanti Kingdom
14. Keys
15. Missing Pieces
16. Opening My Heart
17. Trophy
18. Deaf Ears
19. Drift Off
20. Night To Morning
21. Time
22. Catch Her If You Can
23. Essence
24. Vitality Wellness
25. Miles Away Love
26. Submission
27. Down For The Ride

28. Bees In The Trap
29. Water
30. Argumentative Pervert
31. Frontal Lobe
32. Creez With The Creez
33. A Stoney Exhibition
34. City Of Sisterly Affection
35. Pattern Of Our Love
36. Knowing Thy Self
37. Promise To Future Wife
38. Animal In Man
39. Bless Up
40. I Will Never Forget You

I Ain't No Poet

Only here to express those raw emotions
I do not have poet friends
My comrades heckle the host of the open mic

Remember He Said

My daddy left when I was eight
The world I began to fight
Little curly head nigga better think twice
His voice in my head
Pain in my heart
Nut up real quick
Never do the joking
Making examples
He told me niggas watching

Holler To The Mountain Top

Found myself in the house alone
screaming to the top of my lungs
The weight on my shoulders had
become too much to bear
Took it all on after emotions were felt
and let go

Have Mercy

On my knees
Too many sins
I am begging God
Please forgive a flawed soul
I want to love myself
Grant me grace

The Letter P

Through my pain I found my purpose
My purpose led me to peace
The land of peace granted me
prosperity

Pretty Tony

Suede navy blue Clark Wallabees
My fly-ness takes her to another stratosphere
Understanding my mantra
Cooler than your favorite poet
Run and gun shooter like contra
No shots missed
Painting vibrant art on her mental
Sentimental mood John Coltrane
Tripping over my style
She caught the munchies for the groovy

Words From The Homey

You reaching genius level
Drawing inspiration from the times
Isaac Newton in quarantine

Real Nigga Poetry

With my legacy in my eyesight
Money piling up on my mental
Grab my pen to write another poem
I appreciate those Amazon royalty checks but I blow those

Father Figure

My role model was the dope man
Was told it is better to be like Mike
How can you tell a young
impressionable mind not to be like his
daddy

Manhood

Now you are wishing I was a square
You cannot un-teach the learnings
Acknowledge the learned behavior
Raising a boy at a young age
Immature lessons

Follow Through

The world is fucked up
Will not find me where I started at
Sore loser
Push the line for the wins
Do not get in my way

Baptized In Lake Minnetonka

Smoking heavy out the pound
The past does not hurt anymore
Demons think they have a hold
Dispelled those negative forces
Spiritual bath cleansing
Dipped in Holy Water
So fresh so clean

Ashanti Kingdom

Iced out the wings on my angel
The guardian shining under the lights
Spending lavish
Never living a life of average
African gold
King me

Keys

Take a few chances
There is no backwards dancing
Unlock the door to advancing

Missing Pieces

Ran into a couple soul mates
Chunks of my heart missing
How can I give you my whole

Opening My Heart

I will follow you to the moon
Yesterday I was scared
Today I let go of the fears

Trophy

All she wanted was to be seen
Asking to be heard was a push
She dated a man with no eyes or ears

Deaf Ears

Expressed I have not been feeling like
myself
Call out for help was ignored
Now you are saying you cannot believe
I took my life

Drift Off

I fell in love with you last night
Soul snatched through eye contact
Spirit lifted from my physical body
after climax

Night To Morning

Gripped in the arms of a Pisces man
Full-blown orange skies
Wonder world nightly wonders
Desires wished upon sparking stars
In the land where dreamers dream
Calls being answered from the callers
of love fulfilled
Wealth and health followed
On a pathway to a Pisces rising

Time

Four days of bliss
Sitting on a cloud is quite comfy
On the fifth day she waved from her
window seat

Catch Her If You Can

She was a star shining when the sun was out
Something you do not see twice
Blessed if given the chance to encounter her

Essence

Power to heal or irritate
Keep the sexual polarity in order
Masculine and feminine balance is key

Vitality Wellness

She massage my whole body
Put CBD on my spirit
A love that heals shattered souls

Miles Away Love

Thoughts of the last vacation
Totally impatient when it comes to
seeing you
So far away
Distant lover
Surviving the weather
Replaying scenarios of our times
together
Holding on to that energy for dear life

Submission

Kisses on your nose
Under my care let go of the worries
Fall into the calmness of my direction

Down For The Ride

Just want someone to hold my hand
Fail or succeed
If I never make it will you still be proud
of me

Bees In The Trap

Emotions to the side
Money on the line
Answer on the first ring
Attracting not chasing
Honey on my stick

Water

Your soft soul touches me deeply
Floating in your ocean
I would not mind drowning

Argumentative Pervert

Like to tell you slick shit
Just want to see you walk away
That booty is amazing

Frontal Lobe

She likes to stay in control
Letting her body go does not come natural
Legs tense during penetration
Kiss on the forehead
Electric Tranquility

Creez With The Creez

Wake up on that fly shit
Impeccable style
Handsome black and flashy
Shea butter having skin glistening
After the compliments of the black seed
oil soap wash down
You never felt this fresh
So gracious
So divine
This creez is in me not on me
Smell me
Effortless with the methodology
Momma I dress myself
Pops bless me with the genes

A Stoney Exhibition

Her body was an open canvas
Walking display of an art gallery
Awaiting the moment to trace her ink

City of Sisterly Affection

Straight out of Philly
I was drawn from the door
Real soulful loving Jilly of the block vibe
Musiq Soul Child wrote "A Girl Next Door" about this jawn

Pattern of Our Love

Met her on a carousel
Trips around the world
She makes me go round and round

Knowing Thy Self

Purpose is the intention behind every calculated move
Watch me groove
Not a word spoken
Fill the room with presence
The essence of divine masculinity
Validity, none needed
Greeted with heavy confidence
Thin line between arrogance
Just sure of the choice of the fork in the road
Awesome blessings bestowed

Promise To Future Wife

Promise to let the pain of the past go
Promise to give you every bit of love I have
Promise to make it last forever

Animal In Man

Reading from the book of capitalism
Either you sink or swim
This the game we in
Do not blame me
Adapting to my environment
Jungle rules
The weak gets ate
Lion tatted on my chest

Bless Up

Such a natural beauty
Divine femininity
Presence exudes positive vibrations
Comforting energy
Lay my head on her pillow
Keep them blessings in her heart for me

I Will Never Forget You

On a journey to a place unknown
Because of that I could not ask you to follow
It was an absolute pleasure to know your name

P.O.E.T.S.

Put On Earth To Speak

www.ingramcontent.com/pod-product-compliance
Lightning Source LLC
Chambersburg PA
CBHW030516220526
45464CB00006B/2814